HOW CAN
JUSTIFICATION
MAKE ME JOYFUL?

✖CULTIVATING BIBLICAL GODLINESS

Series Editors
Joel R. Beeke and Ryan M. McGraw

Dr. D. Martyn Lloyd-Jones once said that what the church needs to do most of all is "to begin herself to live the Christian life. If she did that, men and women would be crowding into our buildings. They would say, 'What is the secret of this?'" As Christians, one of our greatest needs is for the Spirit of God to cultivate biblical godliness in us in order to put the beauty of Christ on display through us, all to the glory of the triune God. With this goal in mind, this series of booklets treats matters vital to Christian experience at a basic level. Each booklet addresses a specific question in order to inform the mind, warm the affections, and transform the whole person by the Spirit's grace, so that the church may adorn the doctrine of God our Savior in all things.

HOW CAN
JUSTIFICATION
MAKE ME JOYFUL?

DANIEL R. HYDE

REFORMATION HERITAGE BOOKS
GRAND RAPIDS, MICHIGAN

How Can Justification Make Me Joyful?
© 2017 by Daniel R. Hyde

Reformation Heritage Books
2965 Leonard St. NE
Grand Rapids, MI 49525
616-977-0889 / Fax 616-285-3246
orders@heritagebooks.org
www.heritagebooks.org

Printed in the United States of America
17 18 19 20 21 22/10 9 8 7 6 5 4 3 2 1

ISBN 978-1-60178-545-9

For additional Reformed literature, request a free book list from Reformation Heritage Books at the above regular or e-mail address.

Before justification we have no right to joy;
and after it no reason for misery.

—John Angell James (1785–1859)

HOW CAN
JUSTIFICATION
MAKE ME JOYFUL?

When I was about twenty years old, I was at a point of spiritual despair. I had been converted during my high school years while attending a Foursquare Church, and now I was a student at an Assemblies of God college and had become disillusioned. I never lost faith in Christ, but I lacked assurance and stability. Thus I began a spiritual exploration and changed my major from accounting to psychology to religion in order to find answers. I took courses on major religions such as Buddhism, Hinduism, Islam, and Judaism; read all the holy books; and went to various places of worship so that I could ask questions.

While exploring these religions, I began reading the Bible voraciously. Everything I was reading and discussing drove me to the Word of God and, thankfully, my Lord and Savior preserved me through those years. When I had opportunity to hear Professor Ronald Wright (1930–2002) lecture, I began to ask questions. Professor Wright gladly took me to his office and said, "Danny, the questions you are asking have all been answered." This Pentecostal minister led me to the Reformation. When I asked him how I could know if I was really saved, he answered, "Have you heard of Martin Luther?" During the next couple of years, I read many major works of the Protestant Reformation.

One day in class, Professor Wright wrote the words of Westminster Larger Catechism, question 70, on the whiteboard:

> Q. 70. What is justification?
>
> A. Justification is an act of God's free grace unto sinners, in which he pardoneth all their sins, accepteth and accounteth their persons righteous in his sight; not for any thing wrought in them, or done by them, but only for the perfect obedience and full satisfaction of Christ, by God imputed to them, and received by faith alone.

As I frantically copied these words, I found the answer I needed in the finished work of Christ. I learned how the biblical doctrine of justification could bring me "the joy of the LORD" and spiritual strength (Neh. 8:10). I want you to know this as well.

What is joy? Joy is not the fleeting emotion of our sinful flesh, but a firm peace from the Spirit (Gal. 5:22). Joy is not a quantity of enthusiasm, but a quality of existence. Joy can be expressed by singing (Ps. 105:43; Isa. 35:10) or dancing (Jer. 31:13), but these are not the only ways of expressing it. This peaceful quality is produced in a child of God by divine truth.

Justification is one such truth. By it, we count ourselves happy because God has been happy to impute to us Christ's righteousness.[1] Our status of joy in Christ leads to our experience of rejoicing in Christ.

THE JOY OF BEING IN JESUS

Justification in Christ has gripped the hearts of God's people for generations, increasing their joy, and it should produce joy in you as well. Our Protestant forefathers said that justification was the doctrine upon which the church stands or falls, and it is like a hinge that opens the door to true religion. When it is lost, reformation needs to happen; when it is upheld, reformation and revival often occur. Without this hinge, the door into eternal life is not opened to the world. No eternal life, no true joy.

The doctrine of justification is vital to our Christian experience. Notice the verbs the Larger Catechism uses, which point to God's activity rather than ours: He *pardoneth* our sins; He *accepteth* us; He *acccounteth* us; and He *imputes* to us. What does He impute? Two nouns answer this question: Christ's perfect *obedience* and Christ's full *satisfaction*.

The only verb the catechism uses that we are the subject of is "received." God does not look on our faith and accept us because of it. We are accepted

1. Pietro Martire Vermigli, *Most Learned and Fruitfull Commentaries of D. Peter Martir Vermilius Florentine, Professor of Divinitie in the Schole of Tigure, Upon the Epistle of S. Paul to the Romanes* (London, 1568), 98.

by His free grace in Christ alone. Our faith merely receives Christ and His benefits, which alone save us.

The doctrine of justification grips our hearts because the holy God forgives us freely and accounts us righteous. He accepts us with our sin, in full view of our transgressions and utter failures. He imputes Christ's righteousness to the unrighteous: "But to him that worketh not, but believeth on him that justifieth the ungodly, his faith is counted for righteousness" (Rom. 4:5). The kind of person whom God justifies is "ungodly" and "worketh not," but he rests on the Lord alone.

This is why in Philippians 3 the apostle Paul describes justification as vital to a joyful life. While recounting his experience before and after justification, he calls us to "rejoice in the Lord" (Phil. 3:1). He calls us to imitate him (Phil. 3:17) in the following way:

> I count all things but loss for the excellency of the knowledge of Christ Jesus my Lord: for whom I have suffered the loss of all things, and do count them but dung, that I may win Christ, and be found in him, not having mine own righteousness, which is of the law, but that which is through the faith of Christ, the righteousness which is of God by faith. (Phil. 3:8–9)

With all his heart, Paul exclaims that he wants to "be found in [Jesus], not having mine own righteousness, which is [from] the law, but that which is through the faith of Christ, the righteousness which is [from] God by faith" (Phil. 3:9). John Owen once said that in this passage Paul deals with justification with "greater earnestness and vehemency of spirit than ordinary."[2]

THE JOY OF LOSS

We experience the joy of justification because of what we lose. Remember that in justification we are passive but God is active. He reckons us righteous while we receive His gift. In response, Paul is enlivened. As a new creature who has been justified, he desires to lose more and more of his sinful self. Here is the mystery of being simultaneously saint and sinner. While Paul already has been "found in [Christ]," he says that he desires more and more to "be found in him" (Phil. 3:9) by losing himself more and more.

Earthly Confidence

There is joy in losing earthly confidence. We "have no confidence in the flesh" (Phil. 3:4)—that is, in our own achievements. Another way of saying it is that we increasingly put no confidence in ourselves. There is great joy in letting go of earthly pride and conceit. In Philippians 3, Paul lists his pedigree and then rejects it:

2. John Owen, "The Doctrine of Justification by Faith, through the Imputation of the Righteousness of Christ; Explained, Confirmed, and Vindicated," in *The Works of John Owen*, ed. William H. Goold (1850–53; repr., Edinburgh: Banner of Truth, 1990), 5:364.

- "Circumcised the eighth day" according to God's law (v. 5).

- "Of the stock of Israel," God's covenant people (v. 5).

- "Of the tribe of Benjamin," one of the tribes of God's chosen people (v. 5).

- "An Hebrew of the Hebrews" (v. 5).

- He looked on his life from the vantage point of "the law, a Pharisee," one of those separated out or cut off from the rest and the holiest of the holy people of God (v. 5).

- "Concerning zeal," as one of those specialized class of zealots, his life was devoted to "persecuting the church" (v. 6).

- As "touching the righteousness which is in the law, blameless" (v. 6).

He says, in effect, "I have lost all confidence in myself; I have been forgiven of boasting, arrogance, and pride." Now he wants to lose more and more confidence in these things and say, "My richest gain I count but loss, and pour contempt on all my pride."

We struggle with arrogance, boasting, and pride in our lives. By grace, we give our lives to Jesus Christ, and He amazingly accepts us, forgives us, pardons us, and imputes to us His own righteousness. Yet our sin nature persists and bubbles up from deep within. Little by little, it leads us to take pride in ourselves for what we have become. We might even begin to pray like the old Pharisee, "God, I thank thee, that I am not as other men are" (Luke 18:11). Maybe you have not been tempted to pray that way—yet. Be on guard against it.

Earthly Gain

There is joy in losing supposed earthly gain: "But what things were gain to me, those I counted loss for Christ.... I count all things but loss for the excellency of the knowledge of Christ Jesus my Lord... [I] do count them but dung, that I may win Christ" (Phil. 3:7–8). All the prestige and power Paul thought he earned he now considered as loss and as dung— good only for throwing in the trash heap outside the city.

Paul's desire was to lose all confidence that there was anything in him that distinguished him from the world in God's eyes. One help against this attitude is self-examination, as we consider ourselves in light of Scripture. We must ask ourselves whether we are willing to give up prestige and status before the world so that we might "win Christ" (Phil. 3:8). If there is anything about your former life that made you something in the eyes of the world, then you must die to it. Consider it trash. Our Lord taught this to His disciples when He said, "He that loveth father or mother more than me is not worthy of me: and he that loveth son or daughter more than me is not worthy of me.... He that findeth his life shall lose it: and he that loseth his life for my sake shall find it" (Matt. 10:37–39). Jesus uses extreme and absolute terminology. You must either place confidence in yourself or in boasting in Christ.

Earthly Righteousness

There is also joy in losing earthly righteousness: "not having mine own righteousness" (Phil. 3:9). We need to lose continually our sense of self-righteousness. We've come to Christ, and we've received Him. Paul warns that the sinful nature within us will tempt us to have a self-righteous spirit that craves to think we are righteous in ourselves.

Righteousness means simply doing right. Paul says that we can try to stand before God in two ways. One way is coming to God with lots of stuff in our hands. You might try adding up all the good things you do and coming to God with your list as if it made you right. That is having your "own righteousness, which is [from] the law" (Phil. 3:9).

The other way to come to God is with empty hands: "not having mine own righteousness, which is [from] the law, but that which is through the faith of Christ, the righteousness which is [from] God by faith" (Phil. 3:9). We come with empty hands to receive what God has given to us in and through Christ. Paul understood the righteousness that God is, and he could never measure up to it. This is why he recognized his need to look at all the things he had done and "count them but dung" (Phil. 3:8). Are you able to say, "All my earthly achievements, all my earthly status, any earthly righteousness—I give it all up "that I may win Christ, and be found in him" (Phil. 3:8–9)? It is a joy to do so.

THE JOY OF GAIN

Paul concludes with a contrast between hating self and loving Christ. The joy of justification in Jesus is that it leads us to rejoice that what we gain is Him. He is of infinite worth and value in comparison to all we could gain. His kingdom is like a pearl of great price, which is worth selling all to gain (Matt. 13:45–46). The kingdom is such because of its King, who is beautiful beyond description, too marvelous for words, too wonderful for comprehension. We've given up all that we have to buy that one pearl, and, having it, we joy in it alone. In contrast to having confidence in ourselves and the things of this life, we have "counted [them] loss for Christ.... For the excellency of the knowledge of Christ Jesus my Lord... that I may win Christ" (Phil. 3:7–8).

Do you see why Paul can boast in Jesus Christ—not in himself? Do you see why Paul, with such vehemence and zeal and urgency, describes to us this gospel? Do you see why he turns away from his own life and his own desires and loves? It is because in this gospel a great exchange occurs: Paul's sins—and ours—are exchanged for Christ's righteousness. In this gospel I lose myself, but I lose myself to find myself truly "in him" (Phil. 3:9) and His righteousness. This leads to true and lasting joy.

Nothing in my hand I bring,
Simply to Thy cross I cling;
Naked, come to Thee for dress;
Helpless, look to Thee for grace;
Foul, I to the fountain fly;
Wash me, Savior, or I die.

THE JOY OF GRACE

During my college years, I had tried to recover the joy of the Lord that I had when I was converted, but I tried to find it in intellectualism instead of in Christ. I also tried to find it in experientialism with the Pentecostal experience. But none of this availed until I learned that my once-for-all justification and my joy as a Christian were rooted in God's gift of Jesus Christ to me.

We learn this when Paul says we are "justified freely by his grace through the redemption that is in Christ Jesus: whom God hath set forth to be a propitiation through faith in his blood" (Rom. 3:24–25). Christ forgave my sins and reckoned His own obedience to me. This is the heart of justification, the fountain of joy: to be stripped naked of all my self-woven rags of works and to stand before God dressed in Christ's righteousness. When Paul says this is by God's grace, he means it. God doesn't give to us part of Christ, leaving us to work out the rest. This imputation of Christ's righteousness is why David sang, "Blessed is he whose transgression is forgiven, whose sin is covered. Blessed is the man unto whom the LORD imputeth not iniquity, and in whose spirit there is no guile" (Ps. 32:1–2).

Note that Paul doesn't merely say that we are "justified…by his grace" (Rom. 3:24). He inserts the word "freely" to show how we are "justified" by His "grace." He heaps up these words to make sure that we never think of justification in terms of our works. Elsewhere Paul asked those who had forgotten they were brought into the church by grace alone: "Are ye so foolish? having begun in the Spirit, are ye now made perfect by the flesh?… He therefore that ministereth to you the Spirit, and worketh miracles among you, doeth he it by the works of the law, or by the hearing of faith?" (Gal. 3:3, 5). Paul contrasts grace and works in justification when he says, "For I testify again to every man that is circumcised, that he is a debtor to do the whole law. Christ is become of no effect unto you, whosoever of you are justified by the law; ye are fallen from grace" (Gal. 5:3–4). If you want to be justified by the works of the Old Testament law, you must keep them flawlessly. It is either works or grace. It is either your obedience or someone else's for you.

The question is not whether we are justified by grace. The question is, how is justification "freely by [God's] grace…without the deeds of the law" (Rom. 3:24, 28)? Westminster Larger Catechism, question 71, states,

> Although Christ, by his obedience and death, did make a proper, real, and full satisfaction to God's justice in the behalf of them that are justified; yet in as much as God accepteth the satisfaction from a surety, which he might have demanded of them, and did provide this surety, his own only Son, imputing his righteousness to them, and requiring nothing of them for their justification but faith, which also is his gift, their justification is to them of free grace.

The Grace of a Surety

Justification makes me joyful when I learn that God has freely given a surety for me. A surety is a substitute who stands in the place of others to do what they cannot do for themselves. What a joy to know that God does not "help those who help themselves," but He helps those who *cannot* help themselves.

We need this because we were "shapen in iniquity; and in sin...conceive[d]" (Ps. 51:5), and we go on to sin in thoughts, in words, and in deeds. We have no chance even to begin to obey God's law perfectly. Instead of being able to cleanse us, the law shows how dirty we are: "For by the law is the knowledge of sin" (Rom. 3:20). Instead of raising us up, the law casts us down. Instead of justification, the law brings condemnation (Rom. 4:15). The law is like a mirror. Are you prepared for what you will see when you look into it? In that mirror we see a reflection of ourselves before God. What we find is, "There is none righteous, no, not one: there is none that understandeth, there is none that seeketh after God. They are all gone out of the way, they are together become unprofitable; there is none that doeth good, no, not one" (Rom. 3:10–12).

Notice the great contrast in Romans 3. As God Himself provides the mirror, so He provides someone to stand in between you and the mirror. Formerly God revealed His perfect righteousness through the law, but now it is through His Son, Jesus Christ, "whom God hath set forth" (Rom. 3:25). There is a great difference between "the law and the prophets" (Rom. 3:21), which revealed God's righteousness through the law to humble the Israelites. Now in the new covenant, God has "spoken unto us by his Son" (Heb. 1:2), the eternal second person of the holy Trinity who has revealed Himself in human flesh "in these last days" (Heb. 1:2).

God graciously "set forth [Christ]" (Rom. 3:25). God sent Christ and provided Him for us. As Paul later asks, "He that spared not his own Son, but delivered him up for us all, how shall he not with him also freely give us all things?" (Rom. 8:32). In His love, God went to such lengths to save us that He did not even spare His only begotten, of whom He said, "This is my beloved Son, in whom I am well pleased" (Matt. 3:17).

God justifies sinners like us by grace because He provided the means of bringing sinners to Jesus Christ. This provision is "unto all and upon all them that believe: for there is no difference" (Rom. 3:22).

As Paul asks, "Is he the God of the Jews only? is he not also of the Gentiles? Yes, of the Gentiles also: seeing it is one God, which shall justify the circumcision by faith, and uncircumcision through faith" (Rom. 3:29–30). No one is excluded from His gracious offer. Since "all the world [is] guilty before God" (Rom. 3:19) and "all have sinned, and come short of the glory of God" (Rom. 3:23), God sent His Son for all—Jews and Gentiles. What a provision of immense love for sinners!

The Grace of Satisfaction
Justification also makes us joyful when we consider that God has accepted His Son's satisfaction for us. When husbands tell their wives, "I love you," they can offer their love with one hand but take back what they promise with the other by holding grudges or by living in unforgiving ways. God doesn't act like that. While it is necessary for us to satisfy the just demands of God's righteousness, we cannot do it. Herein is the length and breadth, the height and depth of the love of God revealed. That which God demands, He provides.

God "set forth" His Son to be "a propitiation" (Rom. 3:25). This involves turning away His wrath from us. A famous bumper sticker says, "Smile, God loves you," but while God is loving, He is at the same time a God of justice who is "of purer eyes than to behold evil, and canst not look on iniquity" (Hab. 1:13). This means that His justice must be satisfied for us to be received into His loving arms. And this is why Paul's statement is so amazing. God put His Son forward as a propitiation, knowing that we are dust (Ps. 103:14). The Son turned away God's anger and wrath, satisfied His justice, and achieved satisfaction for us. The God who demands perfection is the one who satisfies perfection; the God who requires everything of us is the one who gives us all that we stand in need of. When you receive by faith the satisfaction that the Son of God made, God looks on you with an everlasting smile.

THE JOY OF FAITH

We live in a time when many people talk about faith, but they rarely understand it. We have "faith-based" initiatives that blur religious lines and are used by politicians to garner votes. Musicians croon about faith, yet few of their songs define it. Others define faith as mere assent to propositions: as long as we profess and believe certain things are true, we have saving faith. Yet others teach that faith is faithfulness, destroying the distinction between faith and works. Yet Paul stressed vehemently that we are "justified by faith without the deeds of the law" (Rom. 3:28).

We must be clear on the doctrine that we are justified by God's grace alone, through faith alone, in Christ alone. When we are, justification brings us great joy.

A Gift from God

A father once experienced this joy after bringing his helpless, demon-possessed son to Jesus, crying out, "Lord, I believe; help thou mine unbelief" (Mark 9:24). He explained, "I spake to thy disciples that they should cast him out; and they could not" (Mark 9:18). Jesus was his last hope. Our Lord called for the boy (Mark 9:19). Then the father spoke: "But if thou canst do any thing, have compassion on us, and help us" (Mark 9:22). "If you can," he says.

Jesus says, "I am the one John the Baptist declared at the beginning of his ministry to be the Lord Himself: 'Prepare ye the way of the Lord'" (Mark 1:3). "I am the one who overcame the devil after being 'in the wilderness forty days, tempted of Satan'" (Mark 1:13). "I am the one with power over the entire created realm. When there was 'a great storm of wind, and the waves beat into the ship, so that it was now full,' I 'arose, and rebuked the wind, and said unto the sea, Peace, be still. And the wind ceased, and there was a great calm'" (Mark 4:37, 39). "I am the one My disciples 'feared exceedingly, and said one to another, What manner of man is this, that even the wind and the sea obey him?'" (Mark 4:41). "I am the one with power over life and death. I made withered hands stretch" (Mark 3:1–5); "I made the dead alive" (Mark 5:35–42); "I made the deaf to hear, and I make the mute to speak" (Mark 7:32–37); "I make the blind to see" (Mark 8:22–25).

Unknown to this father, Jesus was just transfigured before His disciples (Mark 9:2–13), giving them a glimpse of His eternal glory and majesty. They heard the Father say, "This is my beloved Son" (Mark 9:7)—the Son who had dwelt with the Father from all eternity in perfection and in eternal blessedness and glory. After all this, the father wonders if Jesus can heal his son.

First the father says, "If thou canst" (Mark 9:22). Jesus repeats his words and says, "If thou canst believe, all things are possible to him that believeth" (v. 23), and then the father says, "I believe; help thou mine unbelief" (v. 24). The father's "if" suggests uncertainty, and he is not confident in Jesus because His disciples couldn't do what he needed them to do. What makes the difference so that he begins by crying out "if" and shifts to "I"? It is the gift of faith. Faith does not come naturally from sinners: "There is none that seeketh after God" (Rom. 3:11).

Paul reminded the Philippians, "For unto you it is given in the behalf of Christ, *not only* to believe on him, but also to suffer for his sake" (Phil. 1:29, emphasis added). Paul wrote that both faith in Christ and suffering for Him are divine gifts. Romans 3 contrasts God's grace, which is received "through faith" (Rom. 3:25; see also 22, 28), with the works of the law. God Himself gives the faith that we need to receive Christ, who made satisfaction for our sins so that we can be justified before God. In Ephesians 2 Paul contrasts God's way of salvation, which includes the faith to receive it, with our works, "For by grace are ye saved through faith; and that not of yourselves: it is the gift of God: not of works, lest any man should boast" (Eph. 2:8–9). He gives faith through the preached Word of Christ: "Faith cometh by hearing, and hearing by the word of God" (Rom. 10:17). When Paul asks, "And how shall they believe in him *of whom* they have not heard?" he literally says, "How will they believe in him *whom* they have not heard?" (Rom. 10:14, emphasis added). This means that preaching is not just about Christ, but about hearing Christ.

The father in the story was desperate. He was "convinced of…the disability in himself and all other creatures to recover [his son] out of his lost condition" (Westminster Larger Catechism, Q. 72). No rabbis or religious elites could do it. Not even Jesus's disciples could help him, despite their delegated authority to cast out demons (Luke 10:17–19). We too may feel this father's struggle of faith, for while we teach that faith ought to be assured, we know that faith is mixed with doubts.

A Grasping of God

Even as Christ gave faith to this sorrowful, sinful father, which led him to Christ for help in the first place, we learn that faith requires grasping God's promises for ourselves. Does this mean that faith itself justifies and gives us joy? No, it is not the quantity of faith but the quality of faith that brings salvation in Christ. True faith in Christ justifies whether it is strong or weak, because it is Christ who saves, not faith. Faith receives Christ for justification; faith does not cause justification. Faith "receiveth and resteth upon Christ and his righteousness" (Westminster Larger Catechism, Q. 72). This is why our forefathers described faith in Christ as "the hand...of our soul" (Belgic Confession, art. 35).

Thomas Watson (1620–1686) said that while faith "hath sometimes a trembling hand, it must not have a withered hand; but must stretch forth itself."[3] We come by faith to receive Christ, and though we might have a trembling hand with doubts and fears and unbelief, we must not let those doubts hold us back from Christ. Stretch out your hand and receive God's offer to you of Jesus Christ. George Downame (1560–1634) described faith's role in justification like this: "A small and weak hand, if it be able to reach up the meat to the mouth, as well performs its duty for the nourishment of the body as one of greater strength, because it is not the strength of the hand but the goodness of the meat which nourishes the body."[4] Even a small, weak hand, if it can reach food and put it in the mouth, is effective.

---

3. Thomas Watson, "Of Wisdom and Innocency," in *A Body of Practical Divinity, Consisting of Above One Hundred Seventy Six Sermons on the Lesser Catechism* (London, 1692), 976–77.

4. George Downame, *A Treatise of Justification* (London, 1633), 142.

We who trust in Christ rest and lean on Him, knowing He will carry us through weakness. Faith is a condemned sinner's casting himself on Christ for justification. We receive Him in order to apply Him. Our souls are wounded by sin. Though the guilt of our sins is forgiven in justification, we still have to deal with the practical struggle of those sins in day-to-day Christian living. Having received Christ, we must constantly apply Him to the wounds of our souls. He is the balm of Gilead to make the wounded whole, to heal the sin-sick soul.

We need to apply the balm of Christ to the wound of the power of sin in our lives. This means that we must receive Christ for our sanctification as well as for our justification. We must lay hold of Christ, and particularly of the power that His death and resurrection have over the power of sin. Apply this gospel work to your soul and receive the healing of freedom and liberation.

JOY AMID ACCUSATIONS

Finally, what difference does the joy of justification in Christ, by grace through faith, make in our lives? In Romans 5:1–11 we have a foundational text for theology and piety. All that Paul says here is rooted in the statement, "Therefore being justified by faith" (Rom. 5:1). Justification grants me "peace with God through our Lord Jesus Christ" (v. 1). I, who was once an object of God's wrath (Rom. 1:18), dead in trespasses (Eph. 2:1), and by nature a child of wrath (Eph. 2:3) have received His peace.

Now in Christ I have "access by faith into this grace" (Rom. 5:2). Through Christ crucified I pass through the veil of the heavenly temple, enter the Holy of Holies, and access God's infinite grace (Eph. 2:18; 3:12; Heb. 4:16; 10:19–25). I have access to God on earth, and I will have fuller access to Him in heaven. In Christ I "rejoice in hope of the glory of God" (Rom. 5:2). I will rejoice in Him when I see Him in His glory. This glory of God is our final salvation (Rom. 8:18, 30; 1 Cor. 15:43; Col 1:27; 1 Peter 1:3–9). And although we are now pilgrims on earth, we can confidently ascend to the heavens. I have this future joy in part now. In Christ, I rejoice that I am righteous in Him and that I have nothing to fear in the future, not even "tribulations," which I "glory," or rejoice, in because I know they work "patience… experience…[and] hope" (Rom. 5:3–4). The difference that justification makes in our lives is that we can have joy amid accusations of conscience.

The Accusations against Us

In this life we face many tribulations (Rom. 5:3) by way of spiritual accusations. When Paul asks, "Who shall lay any thing to the charge of God's elect?" he asks so confidently, knowing "it is God that justifieth" (Rom. 8:33).

The world hypocritically accuses us of sin in order to appease itself. Like the woman caught in adultery (John 8:1–12), the world surrounds us with its stones to condemn us. Our indwelling sin clings to us like a "body of death" (Rom. 7:24). The law charges us. Paul says, "The strength of sin is the law" (1 Cor. 15:56). It powerfully declares to us what is right and wrong, that we've not measured up, and that we deserve condemnation. Our own consciences charge us, either accusing or excusing us (Rom. 2:15; 1 John 3:20). The devil charges us. This is why he is called "the accuser of our brethren…which accused them before our God day and night" (Rev. 12:10).

How should we respond to such accusations? The word "charge" refers to a legal accusation in a court. Our enemies all rush forward to the judge's bench, as it were, crowding each other out, fighting over one another, yelling charges against us. Heidelberg Catechism, question 60, says there are three accusations against us.

We are charged with having *"grievously sinned against all the commandments of God."* Because God is righteous and must punish sin, this is a pointed accusation since we deserve God's just condemnation. And since we know this is true of us, we pray, "O my God, I am ashamed and blush to lift up my face to thee, my God: for our iniquities are increased over our head, and our trespass is grown up unto the heavens" (Ezra 9:6).

We are charged with having *"kept none of the commandments of God."* The law, in particular, brings this accusation. It says to us, "It's not good enough for you to say that you have already been declared righteous, because I demand perfect obedience." The law is relentless. It follows us, condemning us, and reminding us of how big a failure we truly are.

We are charged with being *"still inclined to all evil."* "You say you're forgiven, but you don't behave perfectly," says the world. The devil says, "You? A child of God? Have you seen yourself lately?" Even as forgiven sinners, the corruption of sin still clings to us.

Justification's Answer

Paul asks, "What shall we then say to these things?" (Rom. 8:31). The response is, "It is God that justifieth" (Rom. 8:33). When we trust in Jesus, it doesn't matter how fast the world, my sinful nature, the law, my conscience, and the devil can run to God to tell Him what I've done wrong. I do not even need to stand up to defend myself! "It is God that justifieth!" Why can I say this?

The first charge against us, that God will punish us in His perfect righteousness, is answered by Jesus Christ's perfect satisfaction for our violations of His law. Since God is righteous, His justice was already satisfied for us on the cross. And God cannot righteously punish the same sin twice.

The second charge against us, that God demands our perfect obedience where we have none, is answered by Jesus Christ's perfect righteousness. His obedience in our place was sufficient for all the demands that God's righteousness makes. Not only does Jesus's obedience for us satisfy for the evil that we have done but also for the good that we have not done. It is not that Jesus obeyed in your place because you have done a bunch of bad stuff; He obeyed for you in every way that you have not positively fulfilled. His life and death were to satisfy for all your sins of commission—what you actually did—and all your sins of omission—what you have not done.

The third charge against us, that God will expel us from His holy presence because of our clinging residue of sin, is answered by Jesus Christ's perfect holiness. He was conceived by the Holy Spirit in holiness, without sin. His holy human nature was united to the holy and divine Son of God, making him the spotless, pure Lamb of God for our sins. He lived a life of holiness in thought, word, and deed; He shunned all sin, doing all righteousness. And when the devil says, "Look at how vile you are!" you say to him, "My holiness is Christ!"

All this is imputed to you when by grace you trust in Jesus Christ. It is not what you have done, it is what Christ has done that God takes and credits to you. And now you can say with confidence that God looks at you "as if I had never committed nor had any sins, and had myself accomplished all the obedience which Christ has fulfilled for me" (Heidelberg Catechism, Q. 60).

You may object, "My faith is too weak." Christ is stronger. "But I am too sinful." Christ is more righteous. "But I'm struggling too much." Christ has overcome all temptation already. Do you trust in Jesus, though ever so little? Then be at rest in God's promises and His power, not in yourself. Do you want to resist sin, though far too weakly? Do you want to please God, though never as you ought? Know that no weapon formed against you, no accusation against you will prosper because "it is God that justifieth" you, a sinner. Caspar Olevianus (1536–1587) said that we have "much more righteousness in Christ than sin in [ourselves]. Indeed, a Christian has more righteousness than do all the angels in heaven."[5]

Patrick Hamilton (1504–1528) offered a priceless set of contrasts illustrating the differences between the accusatory voice of the law and the comforting voice of the gospel in relation to our justification:

> The Law saith to the sinner, "Pay thy debt." The Gospel saith, "Christ hath paid it."

> The Law saith, "Thou art a sinner, despair, thou shalt be damned." The Gospel saith, "Thy sins are forgiven thee. Be of good comfort, thou shalt be saved."

> The Law saith, "Make amends for thy sin." The Gospel saith, "Christ hath made it for thee."

---

5. Caspar Olevianus, *A Firm Foundation: An Aid to Interpreting the Heidelberg Catechism*, trans. and ed. Lyle D. Bierma (Carlisle, England: Paternoster Press), 119.

The Law saith, "The Father of Heaven is angry with thee." The Gospel saith, "Christ hath pacified Him with His blood."

The Law saith, "Where is thy righteousness, goodness, and satisfaction?" The Gospel saith, "Christ is thy righteousness, goodness and satisfaction."

The Law saith, "Thou art bound and obliged unto me, to the devil, and to hell." The Gospel saith, "Christ hath delivered thee from them all."[6]

When you are accused, tell your accusers that you are a believer in Jesus Christ and that "the poorest believer that is this day in the world, is justified as much as ever the apostle Paul was; and every true believer is as much justified now, as he will be a thousand years hence."[7] As Martin Luther wrote to a former student,

When the devil throws our sins up to us and declares that we deserve death and hell, we ought to speak thus: "I admit that I deserve death and hell. What of it? Does this mean that I shall be sentenced to eternal damnation? By no means. For I know One who suffered and made satisfaction in

---

6. Peter Lorimer, *Precursors of Knox, or Memories of Patrick Hamilton, the First Preacher and Martyr of the Scottish Reformation* (Edinburgh: Thomas Constable and Co., 1857), 110–11.

7. Robert Traill, "Eleven Sermons on Important Subjects, from 1 Peter i.1–4," in *The Works of Robert Traill* (Edinburgh: Banner of Truth, 1975), 75.

my behalf. His name is Jesus Christ, Son of God, and where He is there I shall be also.[8]

CONCLUSION

Thousands of years before I experienced the joy of justification, another sinner, who had been saved but was disillusioned, experienced revival of the joy of the Lord. David committed serious sin, experientially severing his joy in the Lord. After committing adultery with Bathsheba, the wife of Uriah, and for all practical purposes having Uriah murdered (2 Sam. 11), David was confronted by Nathan the prophet, who exposed the king's sin: "Thou art the man" (2 Sam. 12:7). David's prayer of confession for these sins is in Psalm 51. After pouring out his heart to the Lord in confession of his sins, he prayed, "Restore unto me the joy of thy salvation" (Ps. 51:12). David prayed for the Lord his God to *restore* to him the joy of salvation. This means that an ordinary part of the ordinary Christian life is ongoing repentance for sin and revival of our joy.

"Restore unto me," David prayed so personally. Do you feel your need to pray like this? When you do, the Lord renews the joy that is a deep and abiding enjoyment and experience of His saving grace. This joy is so precious to the believer, said David

---

8. "Martin Luther to Jerome Weller, July 1530," in *Luther: Letters of Spiritual Counsel*, trans. and ed. Theodore G. Tappert (1960; repr., Vancouver, B.C.: Regent College Publishing, 2003), 86–87.

Dickson (1583–1663), that "he cannot rest or be quiet till he recover the assurance he had, and his wonted joy be joined therewith."[9]

This joy is of the Lord's salvation. Biblically speaking, salvation is a broad term that encompasses all that God does to bring us from the cesspool of our sins to the Celestial City. Salvation is past, present, and future. God has saved us, God is saving us, and God will save us. He has saved us in our justification, and He is saving us in our sanctification. He will save us in our glorification. I have focused on the joy that the Lord gives us in justification. My prayer is that as you read this booklet you will experience what Isaiah longed to see his fellow Israelites experience:

> I will greatly rejoice in the LORD, my soul shall be joyful in my God; for He hath clothed me with the garments of salvation, he hath covered me with the robe of righteousness, as a bridegroom decketh himself with ornaments, and as a bride adorneth herself with her jewels. (Isa. 61:10)

This biblical teaching of justification brings the joy that God has freed you from sin. When he grasped that Christ's righteousness was what made him acceptable to God, John Bunyan (1628–1688) said, "My chains [fell] off my legs indeed, I was loosed from my affliction and irons.… I also went home

---

9. David Dickson, *A Commentary on the Psalms: Two Volumes in One* (1653–1655; repr., Edinburgh: Banner of Truth, 1995), 310.

rejoicing, for the grace and love of God."[10] I want you to know the peace and joy of justification. As C. H. Spurgeon (1834–1892) said, "Peace is the flowing of the brook, but joy is the dashing of the waterfall when the brook is filled, bursts its banks and rushes down the rocks!"[11]

---

10. John Bunyan, "Grace Abounding to the Chief of Sinners," in *The Works of John Bunyan*, ed. George Offor (1854; repr., Edinburgh: Banner of Truth, 2009), 1:35.

11. C. H. Spurgeon, "Pardon and Justification," in *The Metropolitan Tabernacle Pulpit: Volume 53* (Pasadena, Tex.: Pilgrim Publications, 1978), 416–17.